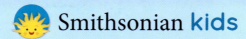

To the Moon and Beyond

Silver Dolphin Books
An imprint of Printers Row Publishing Group
A division of Readerlink Distribution Services, LLC
9717 Pacific Heights Blvd, San Diego, CA 92121
www.silverdolphinbooks.com

Copyright © 2025 Printers Row Publishing Group and the Smithsonian

All rights reserved. No part of this publication may be reproduced, distributed, or transmitted in any form or by any means, including photocopying, recording, or other electronic or mechanical methods, without the prior written permission of the publisher, except in the case of brief quotations embodied in critical reviews and certain other noncommercial uses permitted by copyright law.

Printers Row Publishing Group is a division of Readerlink Distribution Services, LLC.
Silver Dolphin Books is a registered trademark of Readerlink Distribution Services, LLC.

The name of the Smithsonian Institution and the sunburst logo are registered trademarks of the Smithsonian Institution. For more information, please visit www.si.edu

The Smithsonian is the world's largest museum and research complex, dedicated to public education, national service, and scholarship in the arts, Smithsonian sciences, and history.

All notations of errors or omissions should be addressed to Silver Dolphin Books, Editorial Department, at the above address.

For Smithsonian Enterprises:
Avery Naughton, Licensing Coordinator
Paige Towler, Editorial Lead
Jill Corcoran, Senior Director, Licensed Publishing
Brigid Ferraro, Vice President of New Business and Licensing
Carol LeBlanc, President

ISBN: 978-1-6672-0263-1
Manufactured, printed, and assembled in Heshan, China.
First printing, January 2025. LP/01/25
29 28 27 26 25   1 2 3 4 5

Image Credits: Superstock, Inc., istock, Thinkstock, NASA, NASA/JPL-Caltech, Getty Images, Science Photo Library, ESA, PICRYL, krazykiwi

Every effort has been made to contact copyright holders in this book. If you are the copyright holder of any uncredited image herein, please contact us at Silver Dolphin Books, 9717 Pacific Heights Blvd, San Diego, CA 92121.

CONTENTS

 **Space Exploration** 5

 **Apollo 11: Mission to the Moon** 37

 **Artemis: Return to the Moon** 69

 **Mars** 103

A NOTE TO PARENTS AND TEACHERS

Smithsonian Kids All-Star Readers were created for children who are just starting on the amazing road to reading. These engaging books support the acquisition of reading skills, encourage children to learn about the world around them, and help to foster a lifelong love of books. These high-interest informational texts contain fascinating, real-world content designed to appeal to beginning readers. This early access to high-quality books provides an essential reading foundation that students will rely on throughout their school career.

The five levels in the Smithsonian Kids All-Star Readers series target different stages of learning abilities. Each child is unique; age or grade level does not determine a particular reading level.

When sharing a book with beginning readers, read in short stretches, pausing often to talk about the pictures. Have younger children turn the pages and point to the pictures and familiar words. And be sure to reread favorite parts. As children become more independent readers, encourage them to share the ideas they are reading about and to discuss ideas and questions they have. Learning practice can be further extended with the quizzes after each title.

There is no right or wrong way to share books with children. You are setting a pattern of enjoying and exploring books that will set a literacy foundation for their entire school career. Find time to read with your child, and pass on the amazing world of literacy.

Adria F. Klein, PhD
Professor Emeritus
California State University, San Bernardino

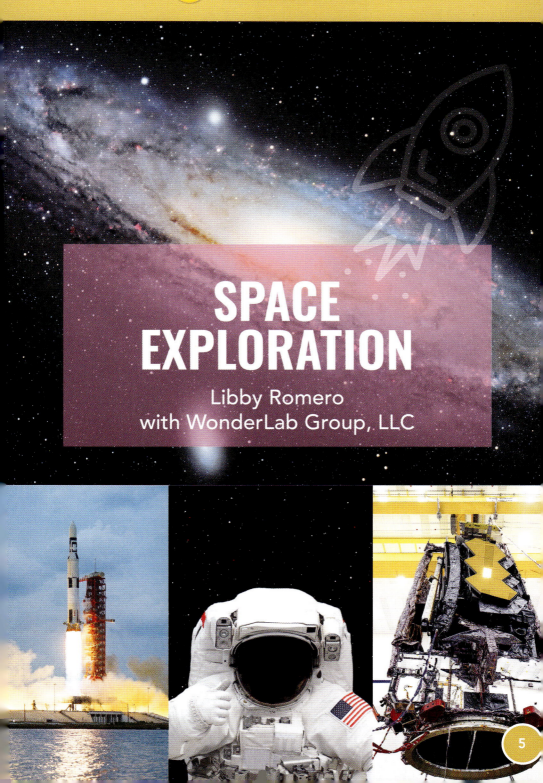

SPACE EXPLORATION

Libby Romero
with WonderLab Group, LLC

Contents

Imagining Space 7
Early Space Exploration 8
The Space Race Begins 10
Humans in Space 12
A Walk on the Moon 14
Rockets and Shuttles 16
Space Stations 18
Telescopes 20
Orbiters and Flyby Spacecraft 22
Landers and Rovers 24
Amazing Discoveries 26
What's Next? 28
Going to Mars 30
Space Explorers 32
Quiz 34
Glossary 36

Imagining Space

Long ago, people looked up at the Sun and the stars. They wondered what was beyond Earth.

Later, **telescopes** helped people see far, far away.

Today, **rockets** can take humans into space. Scientists are still learning more about the mysteries of space.

Early Space Exploration

Astronomers are people who study stars, planets, and space.

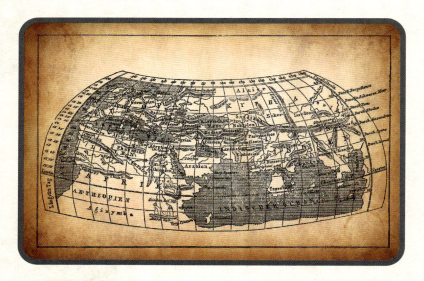

Claudius Ptolemy was a famous astronomer from Rome. Around AD 100, he built a model of the solar system. The model had Earth at the center.

People believed that everything in the sky revolved around Earth. They believed this for over a thousand years.

In 1543, astronomer Nicolaus Copernicus said the Sun was the center of the **universe**.

Johannes Kepler agreed with Copernicus. Kepler discovered how the planets move around the Sun.

In 1609, Galileo Galilei built a telescope. He observed Earth's Moon and Jupiter's moons.

In 1687, Sir Isaac Newton explained that planets orbit the Sun. He called this force **gravity**.

The Space Race Begins

In 1955, the Space Race began.

In the 1950s, the Space Race was between the United States and the Soviet Union.

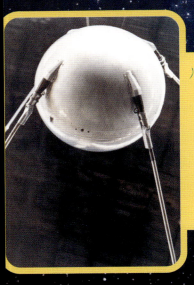

The Soviet Union was the early leader. In 1957, it launched *Sputnik*, the first artificial **satellite** to orbit Earth.

One month later, *Sputnik II* carried a dog named Laika into space.

Soon, the United States' satellite, *Explorer 1*, orbited Earth.

Many people in the United States were worried about the Soviets' success in space.

The United States created a new agency to focus on civilian space exploration. It was called the National Aeronautics and Space Administration (NASA).

Project Mercury was NASA's first human spaceflight program. Its goal was to send people into outer space.

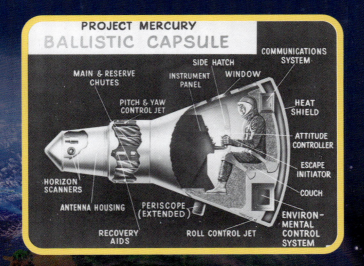

Humans in Space

Project Mercury succeeded. But the Soviets were first to send people into space.

In 1961, Soviet cosmonaut Yuri Gagarin became the first person to orbit Earth.

Three weeks later, **astronaut** Alan Shepard became the first American in space.

U.S. president John F. Kennedy issued a challenge. The U.S. would land a human on the Moon by the end of the decade.

Eight months later, American astronaut John Glenn orbited Earth.

In 1965, cosmonaut Alexei Leonov performed the first **space walk**.

NASA started the Gemini program. Astronauts learned how to dock, or connect, with other spacecraft in space. With Gemini, NASA learned necessary skills for traveling to the Moon.

A Walk on the Moon

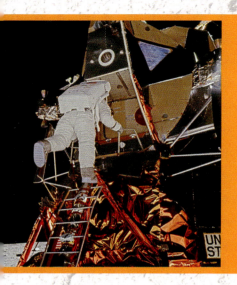

NASA's Apollo program had the goal of landing humans on the Moon.

On July 20, 1969, Apollo 11 landed on the Moon.

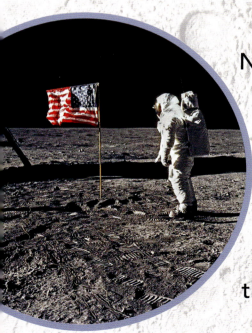

Neil Armstrong and then Buzz Aldrin became the first two people to walk on the Moon. They did experiments, took photographs, and gathered samples from the Moon's surface.

Six Apollo missions landed on the Moon's surface. The astronauts did experiments and brought Moon rocks back to Earth to study.

Apollo 13 ran into trouble. While in space, a tank exploded and damaged the spacecraft.

The astronauts could not land on the Moon. NASA's ground crew and mission control helped get them safely back to Earth.

Rockets and Shuttles

Earth's gravity is strong. It takes a lot of energy to launch an object into space.

That power comes from a rocket.

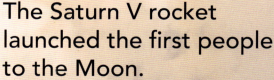

The Saturn V rocket launched the first people to the Moon.

In the 1980s, NASA started using space shuttles.

A space shuttle orbiter launched like a rocket. It landed like an airplane.

Astronauts did experiments on space shuttles.

Space shuttles carried people and supplies into space.

Space Stations

Space stations are giant labs where people can live and work in space.

The Soviets' Salyut 1 was the first space station. It orbited Earth for one hundred and seventy-five days.

In 1973, NASA launched Skylab. From Skylab, astronauts studied Earth and how space affected their bodies.

In 1986, the Soviets launched the Mir space station.

In 1995, cosmonaut Valeri Polyakov spent 437 days on Mir. He set the record for the longest single spaceflight.

Beginning in 1998, fifteen countries worked together to build the International Space Station (ISS). Since then, people from many countries have gone to the ISS.

Telescopes

Telescopes are instruments that use lenses or mirrors. They make faraway objects look bigger and clearer.

Some telescopes are small enough to fit in your hand. Other telescopes are huge!

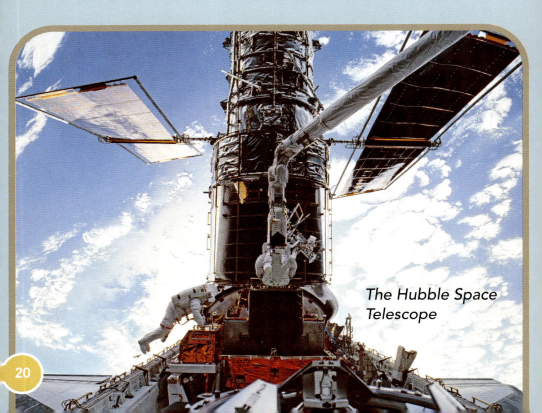

The Hubble Space Telescope

In 1990, the Hubble Space Telescope was launched. It orbits Earth and takes photos of the universe.

The Kepler Space Telescope discovered more than 2,600 planets outside our solar system.

The European Extremely Large Telescope (ELT) will be the biggest telescope on the ground.

Its main mirror is 128 feet across!

The ELT will study stars, black holes, and how **galaxies** change.

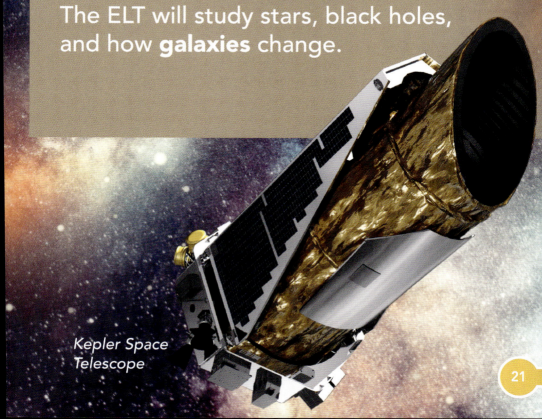

Kepler Space Telescope

Orbiters and Flyby Spacecraft

Orbiters are uncrewed spacecraft. They circle objects in space and collect information that is sent back to Earth.

Mars Reconnaissance Orbiter

The Mars Reconnaissance Orbiter has been orbiting Mars since 2006.

Voyager 1

Voyager 1 and Voyager 2 were launched in 1977. Voyager 1 flew by Jupiter and Saturn. Voyager 2 flew past Jupiter, Saturn, Uranus, and Neptune.

Then they kept on flying—right out of our solar system. They are still flying!

Landers and Rovers

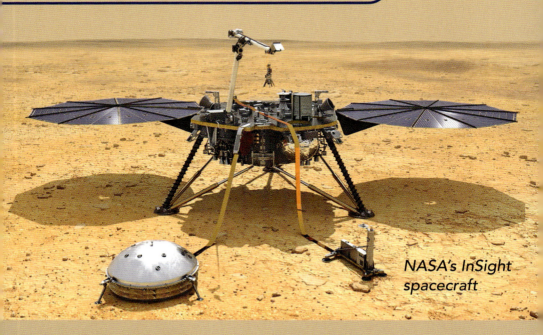

NASA's InSight spacecraft

Humans haven't been to other planets yet. But robotic explorers have. Landers are one kind of robotic explorer.

The lander InSight has been sitting in the same spot on Mars since 2018.

It records everything around it.

InSight's tools have helped scientists understand the structure of Mars.

Rovers are another kind of robotic explorer. Unlike landers, rovers can move.

NASA has sent five rovers to Mars. Rovers have taken photos and tested soil and rocks from Mars's surface.

Some search for water and signs of life on Mars.

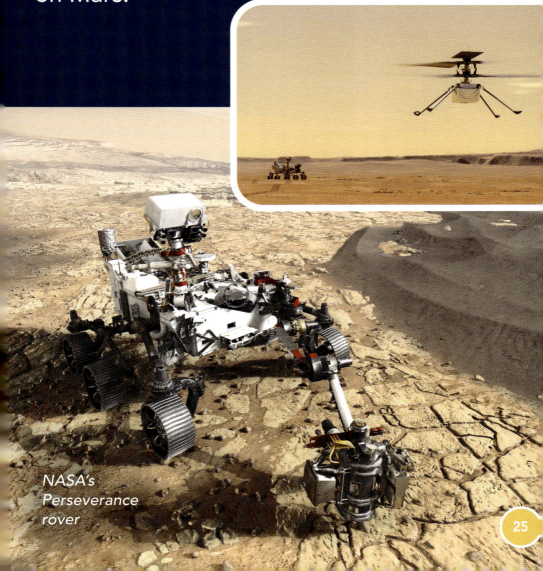

NASA's Perseverance rover

Amazing Discoveries

Thanks to space exploration, we have learned many amazing things about space:

There are more than 200 billion galaxies in the universe.

The universe is getting bigger every second.

Our galaxy, the Milky Way, has a giant black hole in the middle.

There are fiery storms on the surface of the Sun. The blazing particles can blast out from the Sun faster than a million miles per hour.

Exoplanets are planets orbiting stars outside our solar system. Over five thousand exoplanets have been discovered in our galaxy.

What's Next?

In 2021, the James Webb Space Telescope was launched. It is the biggest, most powerful telescope ever launched into space.

The telescope can capture images of the earliest galaxies. It will search for life in other solar systems.

Astronomers will use it to learn more about how the universe formed.

The Artemis program is NASA's plan to go back to the Moon.

It plans to land both astronauts and robotic spacecraft on the Moon.

Astronauts will learn how to live there.

This will help with NASA's next goal: sending astronauts to Mars.

Going to Mars

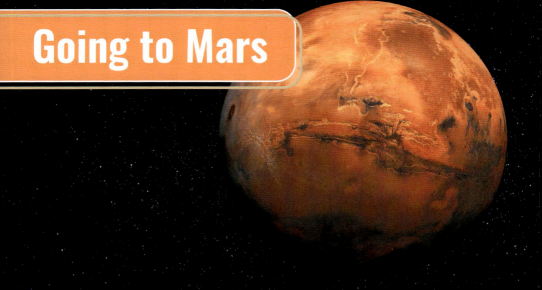

Mars is one of the most explored objects in our solar system.

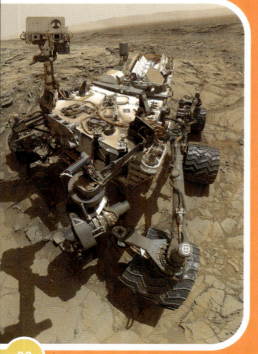

In 2021, several nations sent robotic explorers to Mars.

The robots study the weather and environment.

The answers they find could help humans live on Mars.

Getting to Mars will not be easy.

The journey will take nine months.

People may bring a structure on Mars to live in.

Space Explorers

It takes a crew of people to explore space.

Scientists study planets, weather, and stars.

Engineers design everything from rockets to space suits.

Technicians help engineers and scientists test, install, and repair new products.

Computer experts write software. They study numbers and facts about space.

Astronauts train and prepare for space travel.

Administrators and program managers organize everything so the astronauts can get to space.

It takes a lot of different people to learn about space.

QUIZ: Space Exploration

1. Which astronomer thought Earth was the center of the universe?
   a) Galileo
   b) Copernicus
   c) Ptolemy

2. What was *Sputnik*?
   a) The first dog in space
   b) The first artificial satellite in space
   c) The first mission to the Moon

3. Who were the first two people to step on the Moon?
   a) Yuri Gagarin and John Glenn
   b) Alan Shepard and Michael Collins
   c) Neil Armstrong and Buzz Aldrin

4. Which of these spacecraft was a space station?
   a) Skylab
   b) Voyager 1
   c) Saturn V

5. How are landers and rovers different?
   a) Only rovers go to the surface of a planet
   b) Only landers do experiments
   c) Only rovers can move

6. Which of these space explorers designs rockets and space suits?
   a) Astronauts
   b) Engineers
   c) Scientists

Answers: 1) c 2) b 3) c 4) a 5) c 6) b

GLOSSARY

astronaut: a person whose job is to travel in space

galaxies: massive groups of stars, planets, gas, and dust

gravity: an invisible force that pulls objects toward each other

rockets: tall, thin vehicles shaped like cylinders that launch people or objects into space

satellite: a natural or human-made object that orbits or moves around another object

space walk: activity outside a spacecraft

telescopes: tools that make faraway objects look closer, larger, and brighter

universe: all the space, matter, and energy in existence

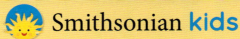

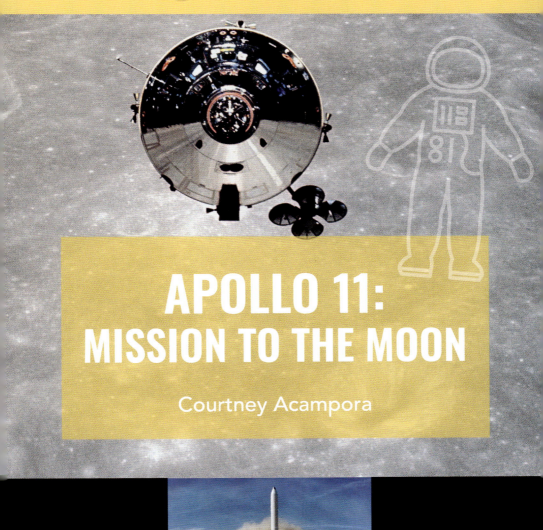

APOLLO 11: MISSION TO THE MOON

Courtney Acampora

Contents

Earth's Moon 39
What Is a Moon? 40
The Space Race 42
NASA 44
Learning About the Moon 46
The Apollo Program 48
Apollo 11 52
The Journey Home 60
After Apollo 11 62
Apollo 11's Legacy 64
Quiz 66
Glossary 68

Earth's Moon

At night, Earth's **Moon** is the largest and brightest object in the sky.

For thousands of years, people stared at the night sky and dreamed of knowing what it was like on the Moon's surface.

In 1969, that dream came true when the first humans set foot on the Moon.

What Is a Moon?

Moons are objects that **orbit** planets.

Some planets have many moons, but Earth has only one.

About every twenty-seven days, the Moon completes an orbit around Earth.

The Moon causes Earth's ocean tides.

Most scientists believe the Moon was formed a long time ago when a large object smashed into Earth.

The collision broke off chunks of Earth that flew into space.

The pieces joined together to form Earth's Moon.

The Space Race

The Space Race was a competition between the United States and the Soviet Union.

Both countries wanted to prove they were capable in space exploration.

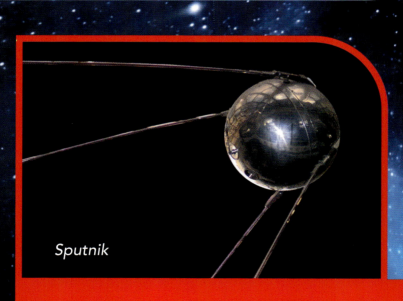

Sputnik

In 1957, the Soviet Union launched the first artificial **satellite**, *Sputnik*.

Yuri Gagarin

Then, in 1961, Russian **cosmonaut** Yuri Gagarin became the first human in space.

He orbited Earth for one hundred and eight minutes.

Because of Gagarin's success, the United States became more determined to beat the Soviet Union in the Space Race.

NASA

After *Sputnik*'s launch, President Dwight Eisenhower signed a law that created NASA in 1958.

NASA stands for National Aeronautics and Space Administration.

NASA is a government agency that focuses on aviation technology and space exploration.

NASA demonstrated the United States' dedication to winning the Space Race.

President Dwight Eisenhower (center)

President John F. Kennedy

On May 25, 1961, President John F. Kennedy requested that the U.S. Congress support a program to land humans on the Moon and return them home safely by the end of the decade.

Learning About the Moon

Before humans could go to the Moon, NASA needed to learn more about it.

They needed to know if it was safe to land machines or humans on the Moon.

They sent **spacecraft** to the Moon that took photos, mapped and tested the surface, and collected soil samples.

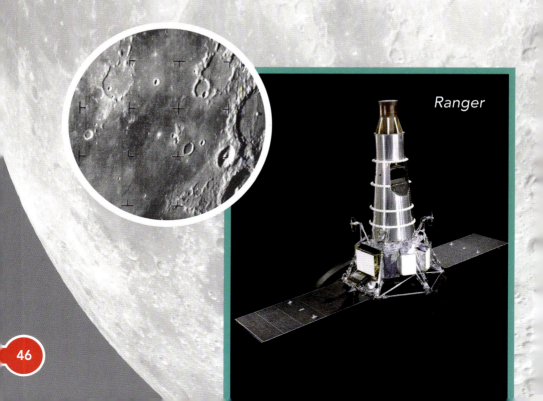

Ranger

Gemini capsule

Project Mercury was NASA's first human spaceflight program. Just one person flew in the tiny Mercury capsules.

Project Gemini followed with a two-person capsule.

Astronauts practiced docking in orbit and learned how to live in space long enough to reach the Moon and return safely.

The Apollo Program

Apollo 1 crew

Several missions happened before Apollo 11.

The first crewed Apollo mission was scheduled for early 1967, but sadly a fire killed the astronauts inside the **command module** during a preflight test.

In 1968, NASA launched Apollo 7.

The crewed command and service module orbited Earth one hundred and sixty-three times and spent more than ten days in space.

The Apollo Program

Apollo 8 was the first mission to carry humans to orbit the Moon and back.

The crew did not land on the Moon, but they were the first people to see Earth from a great distance with their own eyes!

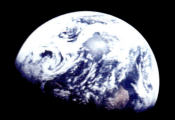

Apollo 9 tested the **lunar module** with a crew in place. The crew orbited Earth for ten days.

Apollo 10 was a complete rehearsal for Apollo 11, but did not land on the Moon.

NASA was ready for Apollo 11—the mission that would land the first humans on the Moon!

Apollo 11

On July 16, 1969, at the Kennedy Space Center in Florida, a Saturn V rocket carrying the Apollo 11 crew took off.

The crew included commander Neil Armstrong, command module pilot Michael Collins, and lunar module pilot Edwin "Buzz" Aldrin Jr.

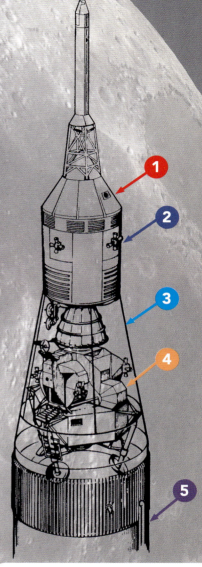

Only three parts of what launched on the Saturn V traveled to the Moon.

The command module, *Columbia*, was the crew's quarters.

The service module held support systems and propelled the craft.

The lunar module, *Eagle*, took the crew to the Moon's surface.

1. Command module
2. Service module
3. Spacecraft/lunar adapter
4. Lunar module
5. Launch vehicle

Apollo 11

Twelve minutes after takeoff, the crew entered Earth's orbit.

They orbited Earth one and a half times.

Then they were boosted out of Earth's orbit toward the Moon.

It took three days to enter the Moon's orbit.

On the afternoon of July 20, 1969, the lunar module detached from the command-service module and began its descent to the Moon.

Apollo 11

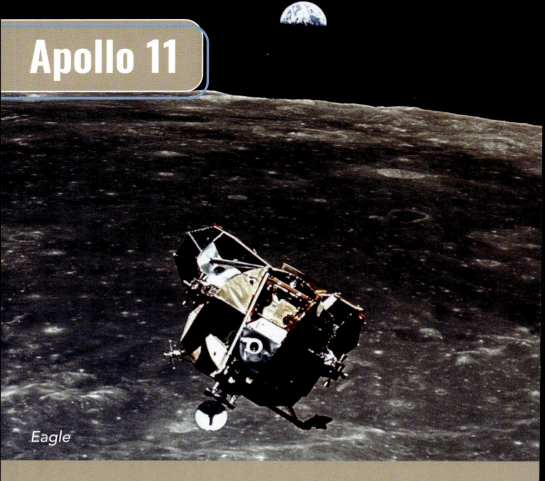

Eagle

Neil Armstrong and Buzz Aldrin landed on the Moon in the *Eagle*.

They landed in a flat area of the Moon called the Sea of Tranquility that was formed from ancient lava flows.

Michael Collins stayed inside the *Columbia* and continued orbiting the Moon.

Before exiting the *Eagle*, Armstrong and Aldrin prepared the lunar module for its stay on the Moon.

The schedule called for the astronauts to rest for five hours after landing, but the astronauts skipped it.

They were ready to step on the Moon!

Buzz Aldrin on the Moon

Apollo 11

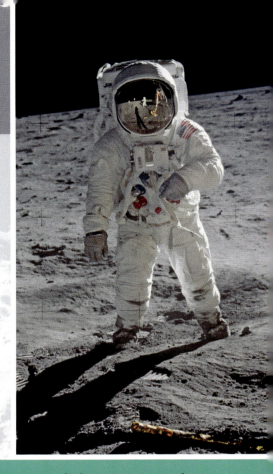

On July 20, 1969, astronaut Neil Armstrong took the first steps on the Moon.

He said, "That's one small step for man, one giant leap for mankind."

Then Buzz Aldrin joined Neil Armstrong on the Moon's surface.

They collected samples, did experiments, and took photographs.

HERE MEN FROM THE PLANET EARTH
FIRST SET FOOT UPON THE MOON
JULY 1969, A. D.
WE CAME IN PEACE FOR ALL MANKIND

NEIL A. ARMSTRONG
ASTRONAUT

MICHAEL COLLINS
ASTRONAUT

EDWIN E. ALDRIN, JR.
ASTRONAUT

RICHARD NIXON
PRESIDENT, UNITED STATES OF AMERICA

The astronauts spent a little more than twenty-one hours on the Moon.

Two and a half hours were spent outside the *Eagle*.

The astronauts left behind an American flag, a patch honoring the Apollo 1 crew, and a plaque.

They left behind their bootprints too!

The Journey Home

Neil Armstrong and Buzz Aldrin took off from the Moon and connected with Michael Collins in the *Columbia*.

The crew left the Moon's orbit on July 21 and landed in the Pacific Ocean near Hawaii three days later.

The crew was taken immediately to a mobile **quarantine** facility. Scientists wanted to make sure the astronauts did not bring Moon bacteria back with them.

After eighty-eight hours inside the quarantine facility, the astronauts were transferred to the Lunar Receiving Laboratory in Houston, Texas.

They stayed there for the remainder of the planned twenty-one-day quarantine period.

After Apollo 11

An astronaut in a lunar rover

After the success of Apollo 11, six more Apollo missions were sent to the Moon.

Apollos 15, 16, and 17 conducted more scientific experiments. They collected samples and explored farther from the lunar module using a Moon car called a lunar rover.

Apollo 13 was unable to land because of a gas tank explosion (but the astronauts made it home safely).

In 1972, Apollo 17 was the last crewed mission to the Moon.

Since then, no humans have stepped on the Moon.

President John F. Kennedy's goal was met.

NASA refocused its work on new technologies and exploring other parts of the solar system.

NASA has plans to send humans back to the Moon in the future.

63

Apollo 11's Legacy

Apollo 11 was important because it showed humanity's ability to go beyond Earth with courage and bravery.

Apollo 11 paved the way for future exploration of even farther reaches of the solar system.

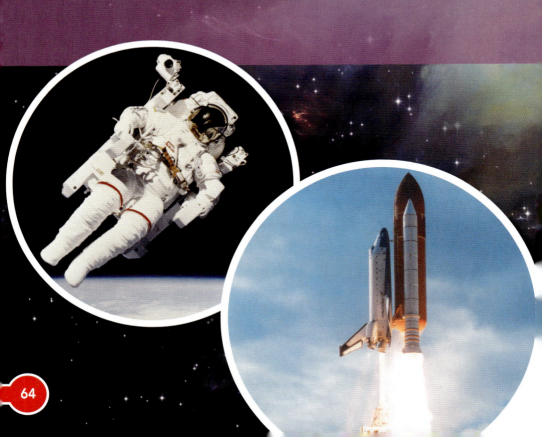

Millions of people watched Neil Armstrong take the first steps on the Moon.

This goal took less than ten years to achieve, and suggests that almost anything is possible.

Apollo 11 has fueled the desire to explore planets, stars, and galaxies far, far away.

QUIZ: APOLLO 11: Mission to the Moon

1. What was the Space Race?
   a) A competition between the Soviet Union and the United States to prove who was the best in space exploration
   b) The launching of two rockets to see which was faster
   c) A race to see how fast Yuri Gagarin orbited Earth

2. What does NASA stand for?
   a) National Aerospace Science Academy
   b) North American Space Association
   c) National Aeronautics and Space Administration

3. Who declared that the United States should land a human on the Moon by the end of the 1960s?
   a) President Dwight Eisenhower
   b) President John F. Kennedy
   c) Yuri Gagarin

4. Where did Apollo 11 launch from?
   a) Florida
   b) Texas
   c) California

5. Which two astronauts were the first to land and walk on the Moon?
   a) Buzz Aldrin and Michael Collins
   b) Neil Armstrong and Michael Collins
   c) Neil Armstrong and Buzz Aldrin

6. What did the Apollo 11 crew *not* leave on the Moon?
   a) American flag
   b) Plaque
   c) Lunar rover

Answers: 1) a 2) c 3) b 4) a 5) c 6) c

GLOSSARY

astronaut: a person whose job is to travel and work in space

command module: the control center and living quarters of a spacecraft

cosmonaut: a Russian astronaut

lunar module: a vehicle for landing on the Moon

moon: a natural satellite that orbits a planet

orbit: to revolve or go around

quarantine: a period of isolation

satellite: a natural or human-made object that orbits or moves around another object

spacecraft: vehicles made for traveling outside Earth's atmosphere

ARTEMIS: RETURN TO THE MOON

Courtney Acampora

Contents

Back to the Moon 71
What Is the Moon? 72
What's It Like on the Moon? 74
History of Moon Exploration 76
Why Go Back to the Moon? 78
What Is Artemis? 80
How Will Artemis Get to the Moon? 82
To the Moon: Artemis II 88
On the Moon: Artemis III 90
Gateway 92
Getting Around on the Moon 94
Artemis Base Camp 96
Moon to Mars 98
Quiz 100
Glossary 102

Back to the Moon

Humans have always wondered what it was like on the Moon.

In 1969, **astronaut** Neil Armstrong became the first person to set foot on the Moon.

The last astronaut to explore the Moon visited in 1972.

No one has stood on the Moon since.

But the Artemis program plans to return astronauts to the Moon!

What Is the Moon?

Moons are objects that **orbit** planets.

Some planets have dozens of moons, but Earth has only one.

Earth's Moon is 4.5 billion years old.

The Moon orbits Earth, and Earth's **gravity** keeps the Moon on its path.

Earth would be very different if it did not have the Moon.

The Moon's gravity limits how much Earth wobbles on its axis.

The Earth's axis is an imaginary line that the planet rotates around.

The Moon's gravity also creates the **tides**.

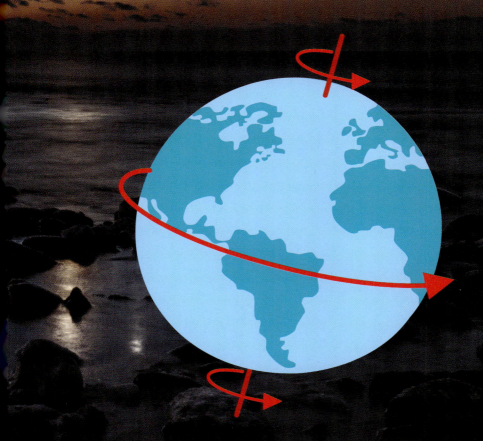

What's It Like on the Moon?

The Moon's surface is covered in craters and **lunar** dust.

The Moon's craters are hollowed-out areas.

They are made from the impact of material from outer space.

Meteors, or space rocks, hit the Moon's surface every day.

Large meteors created the Moon's craters.

The Moon has a very thin atmosphere.

An atmosphere is a layer of gases around a planet or moon.

There is less gravity on the Moon than on Earth. That means astronauts bounce when they walk!

Compared to Earth, the Moon is very hot in the sunlight.

The Moon is very cold in the shade.

It is scorching hot during the day and freezing cold at night.

History of Moon Exploration

In the 1960s, NASA (National Aeronautics and Space Administration) oversaw the Apollo program.

The Apollo program's goal was to land a human on the Moon, and return them safely to Earth.

In 1969, the Apollo 11 mission made history.

It landed humans on the Moon for the first time.

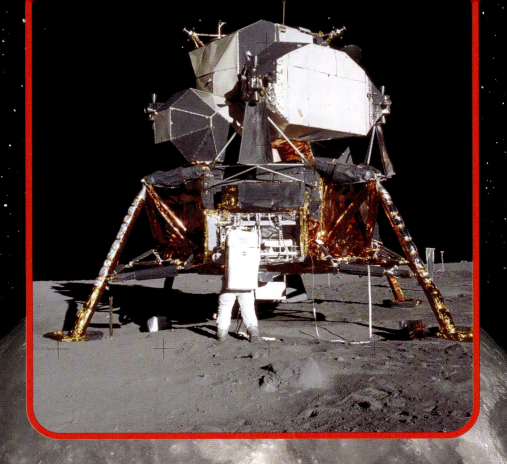

Five more Apollo missions brought astronauts to the Moon's surface.

Apollo 17 was the final mission to the Moon in the Apollo program.

In 1972, the Apollo program came to an end.

Why Go Back to the Moon?

The Moon is the nearest place to Earth to learn about living on another planetary body.

Scientists will test technology and do experiments there.

This will help them predict how technology will work on other planets.

Scientists will learn what it's like to live and work on a place far from Earth.

Artemis missions will allow for new discoveries on the Moon.

The Moon will be used to prepare for a future mission to Mars.

Scientists want to learn if there was once life on Mars.

What Is Artemis?

Humans have not walked on the Moon in over fifty years.

NASA leads the Artemis program that plans to return to the Moon.

Artemis plans to land the first woman and person of color on the Moon.

The goal of the Artemis III mission is to land astronauts on the Moon.

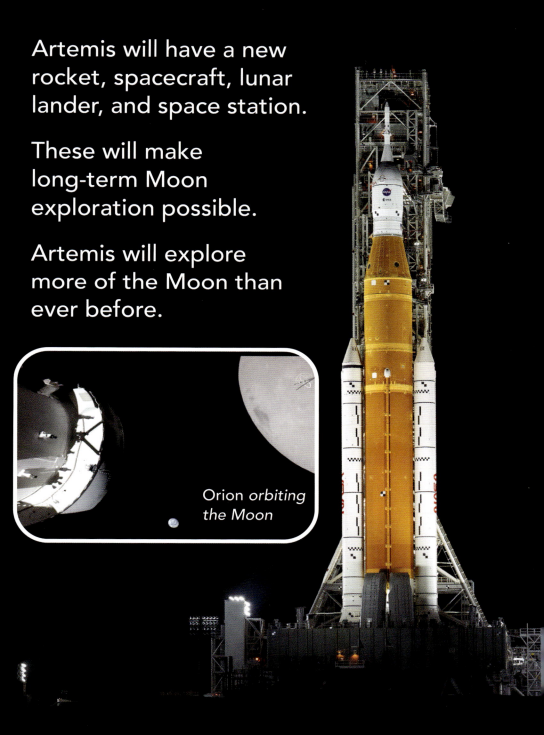

Artemis will have a new rocket, spacecraft, lunar lander, and space station.

These will make long-term Moon exploration possible.

Artemis will explore more of the Moon than ever before.

Orion *orbiting the Moon*

How Will Artemis Get to the Moon?

The SLS (Space Launch System)

The SLS is the **rocket** that is used in the Artemis program.

It is the most powerful rocket NASA has launched.

It will launch the Orion spacecraft to the Moon.

In 2022, the SLS launched Artemis I from the Kennedy Space Center.

Artemis I was an uncrewed trip to the Moon's orbit.

The SLS will be used for future missions to the Moon and Mars.

How Will Artemis Get to the Moon?

Orion

Orion is the spacecraft that will carry astronauts to the Moon's orbit.

It is designed to transport humans farther than they have ever gone before.

Orion will be launched on the SLS rocket.

Orion's crew module is where the astronauts will live and work.

The service module powers Orion and includes life support like water and oxygen.

Astronauts can live on Orion for twenty-one days.

How Will Artemis Get to the Moon?

Human Landing System (HLS)

Orion will dock, or connect, with the HLS in the Moon's orbit.

The HLS will bring astronauts down to the Moon's surface.

The company SpaceX is designing the first HLS. It is called Starship.

The HLS is designed to safely land on the Moon's surface.

Astronauts can live and work in the HLS while on the Moon.

The HLS will protect the astronauts from harmful **radiation**.

It will transport the astronauts to the Moon's surface.

The HLS will take astronauts back to Orion in orbit.

To the Moon: Artemis II

The Artemis II astronauts will go on a ten-day flight to the Moon.

They will perform a flyby of the Moon; they will not land on it.

It will be the first mission with the crew aboard Orion.

The astronauts will see what it's like living and traveling in deep space.

Artemis II Astronauts

First, they will orbit Earth to check Orion's life-support systems.

Then the astronauts will continue their journey to the Moon.

They will do the flyby of the Moon, then will travel back to Earth.

Artemis III will build on the lessons learned from Artemis II.

On the Moon: Artemis III

Artemis III is planned to land humans on the Moon's surface.

Four astronauts in Orion will dock with Starship in the Moon's orbit.

Starship will take two astronauts to the Moon's surface.

The other two astronauts will orbit the Moon in Orion.

Starship will land astronauts near the Moon's south pole. Astronauts have never visited there.

The astronauts will go on **moonwalks** and do experiments.

After around six days, they will get in Starship and reconnect with Orion.

Then they will journey back to Earth.

Gateway

A space station is a place where astronauts can live and work in space.

It includes everything astronauts need to live in space for some time.

A space station called the International Space Station orbits Earth.

Gateway is planned to be the first space station to orbit the Moon.

Gateway will be built after Artemis III.

Artemis IV astronauts will live and work on Gateway.

Gateway will allow for more trips to the Moon's surface.

It will be used as a home base for future missions to the Moon.

Gateway will also be a stopping point on the way to Mars.

Getting Around on the Moon

Space suits

Astronauts will need special space suits to wear on the Moon.

Space suits are clothes and equipment astronauts wear to survive in space.

Space suits have oxygen to breathe and water to drink.

Astronauts can talk to each other using the space suits' communication systems.

Lunar Terrain Vehicle (LTV)

The LTV is a vehicle used on the Moon and other planets.

Artemis astronauts will drive the LTV on the Moon.

The LTV is also a robot that can do experiments.

Astronauts will use the LTV to travel around the lunar surface.

Artemis Base Camp

NASA plans to build an Artemis base camp on the Moon.

It will allow for longer stays on the Moon's surface.

The base camp will include a cabin, rover, and mobile home.

Solar panels could collect energy from the Sun to power the base camp.

There is still much to learn about living on the Moon.

Moon to Mars

Scientists are interested in Mars because life may have existed there.

The Artemis missions to the Moon will be important for space exploration.

They will be used to prepare for future missions to Mars.

To go to Mars, humans will need to learn how to survive far from Earth. Artemis will prepare astronauts to one day live and work on Mars.

It will be many years before humans go to Mars.

But Artemis is an important step toward bringing humans to Mars!

QUIZ: ARTEMIS: RETURN TO THE MOON

1. Why are we going back to the Moon?
   a) For science and to prepare for Mars exploration
   b) To build the International Space Station
   c) To restart the Apollo program

2. What spacecraft will Artemis astronauts use to go to the Moon?
   a) *Voyager 2*
   b) Orion
   c) *Apollo 17*

3. Why do astronauts need space suits on the Moon?
   a) To protect from extreme temperatures
   b) To provide water and oxygen
   c) All of the above

4. What will happen during Artemis II?
   a) Astronauts will visit the Moon's surface
   b) An uncrewed Orion spacecraft will orbit the Moon
   c) Astronauts will perform a flyby of the Moon and test out Orion

5. What is Gateway?
   a) The most powerful rocket NASA has ever built
   b) A space station that will orbit the Moon
   c) A lunar lander that will take humans to the Moon's surface

6. Where will the Artemis base camp be built?
   a) Where Apollo 11 landed
   b) Near the Moon's south pole
   c) The far side of the Moon

Answers: 1) a 2) b 3) c 4) c 5) b 6) b

GLOSSARY

astronaut: a person whose job is to travel in space

gravity: an invisible force that pulls objects toward each other

lunar: of, or relating to, the Moon

moonwalks: time spent on the Moon outside a spacecraft

orbit: to revolve or go around

radiation: energy that moves from one place to another, such as the energy from the Sun

rocket: a powerful vehicle that launches people or objects into space

tides: the rise and fall of the ocean surface that happens twice a day

Smithsonian kids

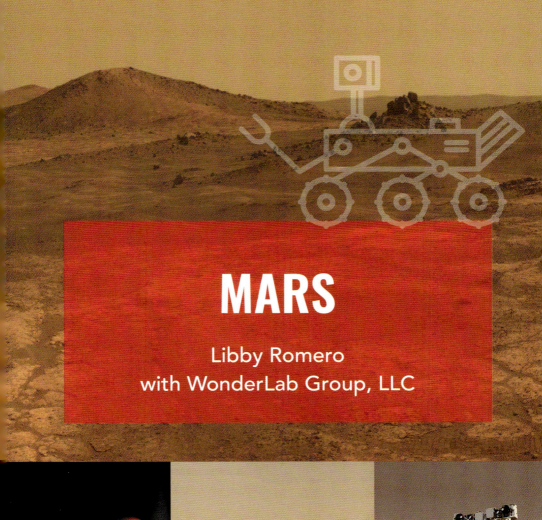

MARS

Libby Romero
with WonderLab Group, LLC

Contents

Meet Mars 105
In the Beginning 106
Distance and Size 108
Time on Mars 110
Seasons on Mars 112
The Moons of Mars 114
A Look Inside 116
Up in the Air 118
On the Surface 120
Extreme Mars 122
Exploring Mars 124
Exploring Mars:
The Twenty-first Century 128
Quiz 130
Glossary 132

Meet Mars

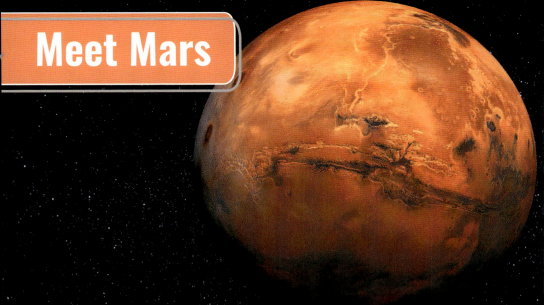

For thousands of years, people have asked questions about the **planet** Mars.

People made up myths, or stories, about Mars.

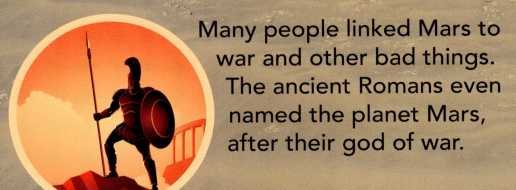

Many people linked Mars to war and other bad things. The ancient Romans even named the planet Mars, after their god of war.

In the Beginning

In 1576, **astronomer** Tycho Brahe looked up at Mars. He tried to figure out how far it was from Earth.

Using math, he came very close—even though **telescopes** weren't invented yet.

In 1609, Galileo Galilei was the first person to view Mars through a telescope.

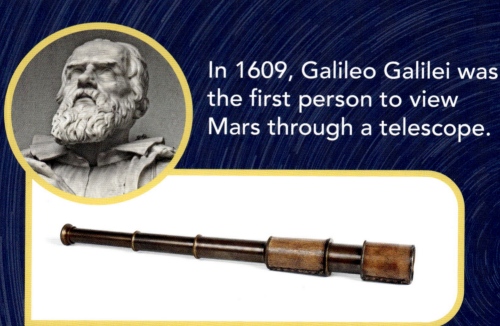

Since then, scientists have studied Mars more than any planet besides Earth.

The solar system formed 4.6 billion years ago. A huge cloud of gas and dust collapsed and spun into a flat disk.

The disk spun faster. Most of the material was pulled into the disk's center.

It created a bulge that formed a star we call the Sun.

The rest of the material spun around the Sun and clumped together.

This formed the planets, including Mars.

Distance and Size

Gravity is an invisible force that pulls objects toward each other.

The more material an object has, the stronger its gravity will be.

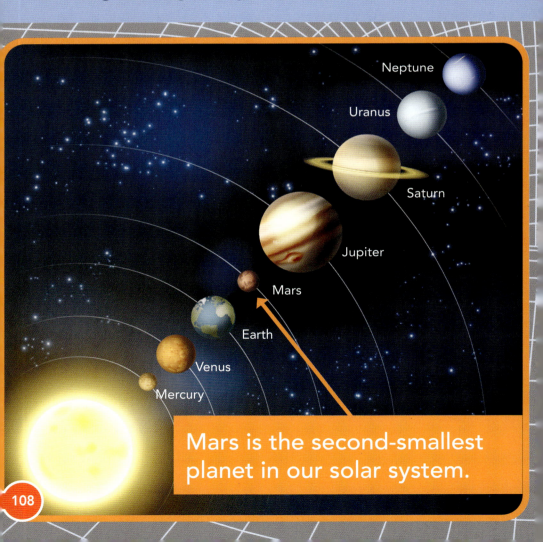

Mars is the second-smallest planet in our solar system.

Mars is about half the size of Earth. It is less **dense**, and has less mass than Earth.

Mars has less gravity than Earth.

A 100-pound person on Earth would weigh thirty-eight pounds on Mars!

Time on Mars

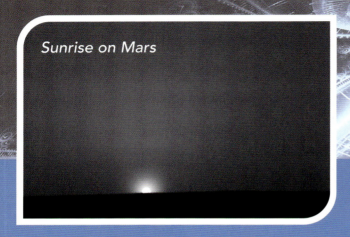
Sunrise on Mars

You can't feel it, but Earth **rotates**.

Mars rotates on its **axis** too.

It takes Mars twenty-four hours and forty minutes to rotate. One rotation is equal to one day.

That's a little longer than one day on Earth.

Sunset on Mars

Mars also revolves, or moves around, the Sun.

One revolution takes almost two Earth years!

It takes so long because Mars's path is more **elliptical** than Earth's.

Plus, Mars is farther from the Sun than Earth is.

Seasons on Mars

Like Earth, Mars tilts on its axis.

The tilt causes the seasons.

A year on Mars is longer than a year on Earth.

So seasons on Mars are longer too.

Winter on Mars

Because of Mars's elliptical orbit, its seasons are different lengths.

Spring and summer are longer in the northern **hemisphere**.

Fall and winter are longer in the southern hemisphere.

Summer on Mars

The Moons of Mars

Mars has two moons: Phobos and Deimos.

Mars's moons were named after the Greek god of war's sons.

Unlike Earth's Moon, Phobos and Deimos are not round.

They're shaped sort of like potatoes.

Phobos is larger than Deimos. It is closer to Mars.

Mars's gravity is pulling Phobos toward it.

Within fifty million years, Phobos will crash into Mars, or Mars's gravity will break it apart.

Phobos's pieces will form a ring around Mars.

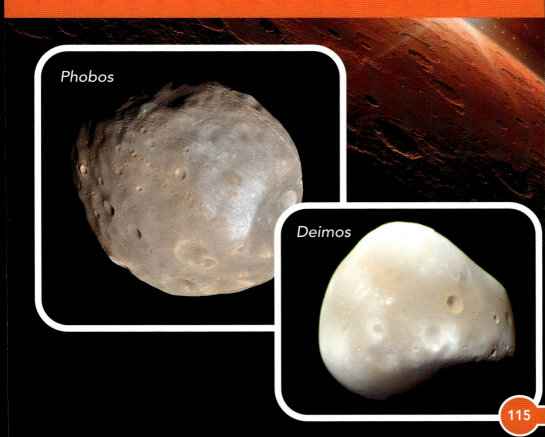

Phobos

Deimos

A Look Inside

The inside of Mars is similar to the inside of Earth.

Like Earth, Mars has a thin, rocky crust.

Mars's crust sits on top of a thick mantle. Its mantle surrounds a metal core.

The crust on Mars is a solid layer. The mantle is made of soft, paste-like rocks.

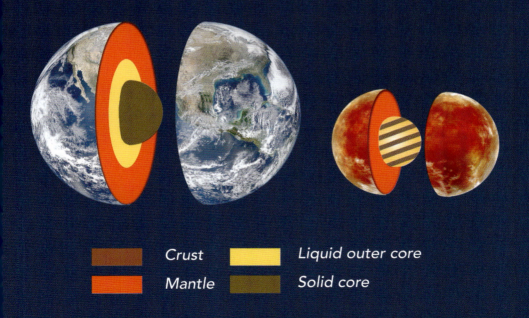

Crust
Mantle
Liquid outer core
Solid core

Scientists don't know if Mars's core is solid or liquid.

There is still a lot to learn about the inside of Mars.

Up in the Air

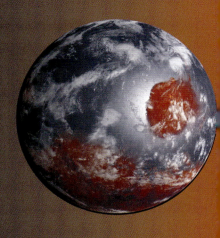

Billions of years ago, Mars was a warm, wet planet.

Like Earth, it had a thick atmosphere, or protective layer of air surrounding it.

Energy from the Sun pushed gases away from Mars and out into space.

The atmosphere became very thin.

Mars's atmosphere could no longer protect the planet.

Today, Mars is cold and dry.

Its thin atmosphere cannot hold heat on the planet's surface.

Temperatures can get as cold as -284 degrees Fahrenheit.

Small blue ice crater

The Serpent Dust Devil

Mars is windy with huge dust storms that sometimes cover its entire surface.

It can "snow" on Mars too.

The snowflakes are made of carbon dioxide. It is the most common gas in Mars's atmosphere.

On the Surface

The surface of Mars is dry and rocky.

There is no liquid water.

But there is ice made from water below the surface and at its poles.

There are also dry lake beds, river valleys, and **deltas**.

These are signs that water once flowed across Mars.

From a distance, Mars looks red.

That's why Mars is called the Red Planet.

Up close, the ground can be brown, gold, and tan.

The red color comes from rocks on the surface.

The rocks are filled with iron.

When iron combines with moisture or air, a red coating is formed.

Extreme Mars

Mars has some giant landscape features.

Volcano

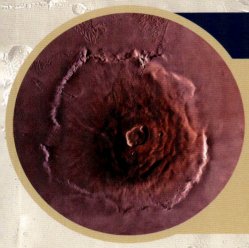

Olympus Mons is three times taller than Mount Everest, Earth's tallest mountain.

Canyon

Valles Marineris is so big it would stretch across the whole United States.

It is six to seven times deeper than Earth's Grand Canyon.

Crater

The Borealis basin is a giant impact **crater** on Mars.

It covers about 40 percent of Mars.

Scientists think a big **asteroid** crashed into Mars and left the crater.

Sand Dunes

A field of sand dunes fills the Russell Crater.

The tallest sand dune is taller than most skyscrapers!

Exploring Mars

Mars has changed a lot since it first formed.

Scientists study Mars to learn about how planets change over time.

This helps them understand how similar changes could affect Earth.

Mariner spacecraft

Early photo of a volcano on Mars taken by Mariner

In the 1960s and 1970s, humans launched Mariner spacecraft to fly by Mars.

These took the first pictures of the planet, and studied its atmosphere.

Viking spacecraft took photos of Mars. These photos helped create the first correct maps of Mars.

Viking spacecraft

Exploring Mars

In 1997, the Mars Global Surveyor (MGS) began circling Mars.

It sent messages back to Earth for nine years.

It searched for signs that Mars once had water.

It succeeded, sending photos of ancient riverbeds back to Earth.

If there was water on Mars, life could have been possible.

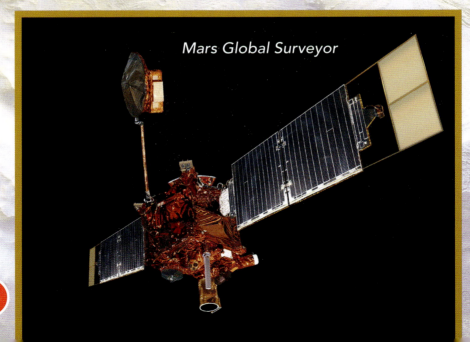

Mars Global Surveyor

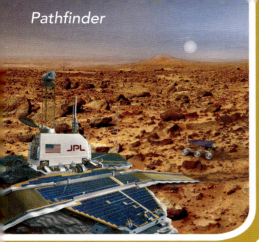
Pathfinder

Also in 1997, the Mars Pathfinder landed on Mars's surface.

The lander carried a rolling robot called the Sojourner **rover**.

Sojourner

Scientists on Earth controlled the rover.

The rover took photos and studied nearby rocks and soil.

Exploring Mars: The Twenty-first Century

In recent years, several countries have sent missions to study Mars.

Today, rovers roll along the Martian surface.

Rovers are like science labs on wheels.

A helicopter drone has even hovered in Mars's thin air.

These robots send data and photos back to Earth.

Ingenuity helicopter

Mars is millions of miles from Earth.

People dream of going there.

They want to build settlements so they can explore Mars up close.

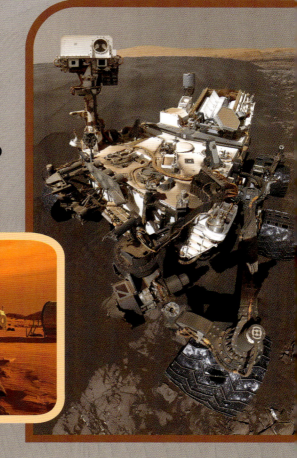

We have learned a lot about Earth by studying Mars.

129

QUIZ: Mars

1. What is Mars?
   a) A star
   b) A planet
   c) A moon

2. How big is Mars?
   a) Bigger than Earth
   b) Smaller than Earth
   c) The same size as Earth

3. What color is Mars?
   a) Blue
   b) Black
   c) Red

4. What is Olympus Mons?
   a) An astronomer
   b) A moon
   c) A volcano

5. Which kind of spacecraft is like a science lab on wheels?
   a) Rover
   b) Orbiter
   c) Lander

6. Which features led to the discovery of water on Mars?
   a) Large glaciers
   b) Ancient riverbeds
   c) Freshwater lakes

Answers: 1) b 2) b 3) c 4) c 5) a 6) b

GLOSSARY

asteroid: a small rocky body that orbits the Sun

astronomer: someone who studies planets, stars, and space

axis: an imaginary straight line that an object spins around

crater: a dip in the ground formed when something hits the surface

delta: a fan-shaped piece of land at the mouth of a river

dense: having parts that are close together

elliptical: oval shaped

hemisphere: half of a planet, divided at the planet's equator

planet: a large, round object that revolves around a star

rotate: to spin, or turn in a circle

rover: a vehicle that explores the surface of a planet or moon

telescope: a tool that makes faraway objects look closer, larger, and brighter